The Adventures of Piper Series
Piper Learns to Serve
(Book 2)

Dave Osborn

The Adventures of Piper Series
Piper Learns To Serve
(Book 2)

© 2024 Dave Osborn

Adriel Publishing

FIRST EDITION

ALL RIGHTS RESERVED. No part of this book may be reproduced in any form or by any means whatsoever, including photography, xerography, broadcast, transmission, translation into any language, or recording, without permission in writing from the publisher. Reviewers may quote brief passages in critical articles or reviews.

Printed in the U.S.A.

Cover design by Book Cover Station

ISBN: 979-8-9900885-6-6

www.DaveOsbornBooks.com

Dedication

This book is dedicated to the healthcare professionals in the thousands of healthcare facilities throughout the country that tend to patients in hospitals, rehab centers, hospice centers, and memory care centers. Their careers are indeed a calling, and therapy animals work together with them as partners to provide another layer of comfort and care for their patients and guests.

More therapy animals are needed, and hopefully this book will encourage animal owners to investigate and pursue this path of service.

Prologue for Parents

In **Piper's Journey Home**, I told the true story of Piper's discovery in the streets and fields of Harlingen, Texas, as a stray puppy. I then related her rescue, adoption, and physical recovery to become a healthy, obedient, and fully socialized pet.

In **Piper Learns to Serve**, my goal is to explain how certain animals – mostly dogs – with good temperaments and obedience skills are needed throughout the country for therapy animal visits in hospitals, hospices, rehab centers, schools, and community centers. The healing effect of personal contact with specially trained therapy animals is remarkable, documented, and is growing.

Piper and I now comprise a "therapy team." We selected Pet Partners as our registration partner because they are national in scope, have a tremendous training and support regimen, and are fully committed to better health through Animal Assisted Interventions, or AAI. Taking a therapy animal into a setting with injured, ill, and/or troubled patients has several types of risks – and Pet Partners does an excellent job of making prospective therapy teams aware of these risks and training them to manage them head on in a professional manner. All Pet Partner therapy teams are volunteers – we do this work because we believe in it - not because there is a paycheck coming.

The Pet Partner registration process is complex and grueling. First, I had to take an 8-hour online course, review the 114-page handbook, then successfully pass the competency exam. Next, I had to have Dr. Shelly Mitchell check over Piper one more time then complete the medical affidavit to include in Piper's registration package. We then found an evaluation center and, after reviewing all the obedience commands that Jaime Benitez at K9 Consultants taught her, we went in and were evaluated as a team. The evaluator paid as much attention to **me** as to Piper to ensure that we were, in fact, operating as a professional team and not putting us at risk once we started making visits.

It has been a lengthy, challenging process, but the payoffs have been worth it. I hope you will enjoy reading **The Adventures of Piper Book 2; Piper Learns to Serve.**

Dave Osborn

Chapter 1
I'm All Grown Up Now!

I don't go hungry any more, and I am very grateful for that.

Dave and Marilyn have taken great care of me, and I'm now a healthy adult dog and no longer a sick, stray puppy!

I have made friends with all the dogs in our neighborhood, and I even have a cat friend that lives next door!

I stay strong with my daily walks with Dave, and I feel good! In fact, I am <u>so</u> healthy that Dr. Shelly told Dave I need to lose five pounds! Dave is a great grill chef, and his spare ribs are wonderful!

Since I am all grown up, Dave wanted to start my special training to become a therapy dog to help people that need the comfort that only a therapy animal can give.

I'm ready now to go through training with Dave and become a therapy dog team! I can't wait to get started!

Chapter 2
Dave Takes His Therapy Dog Training and Test!

The first step was to get Dave approved as a trained therapy animal "handler" or someone who escorts a therapy animal on a therapy visit.

Dave took the training for several hours on his computer and passed his exam on the first try!

Next I went to see Dr. Shelly to get a medical approval to show that I am healthy and able to carry out therapy animal duties with Dave.

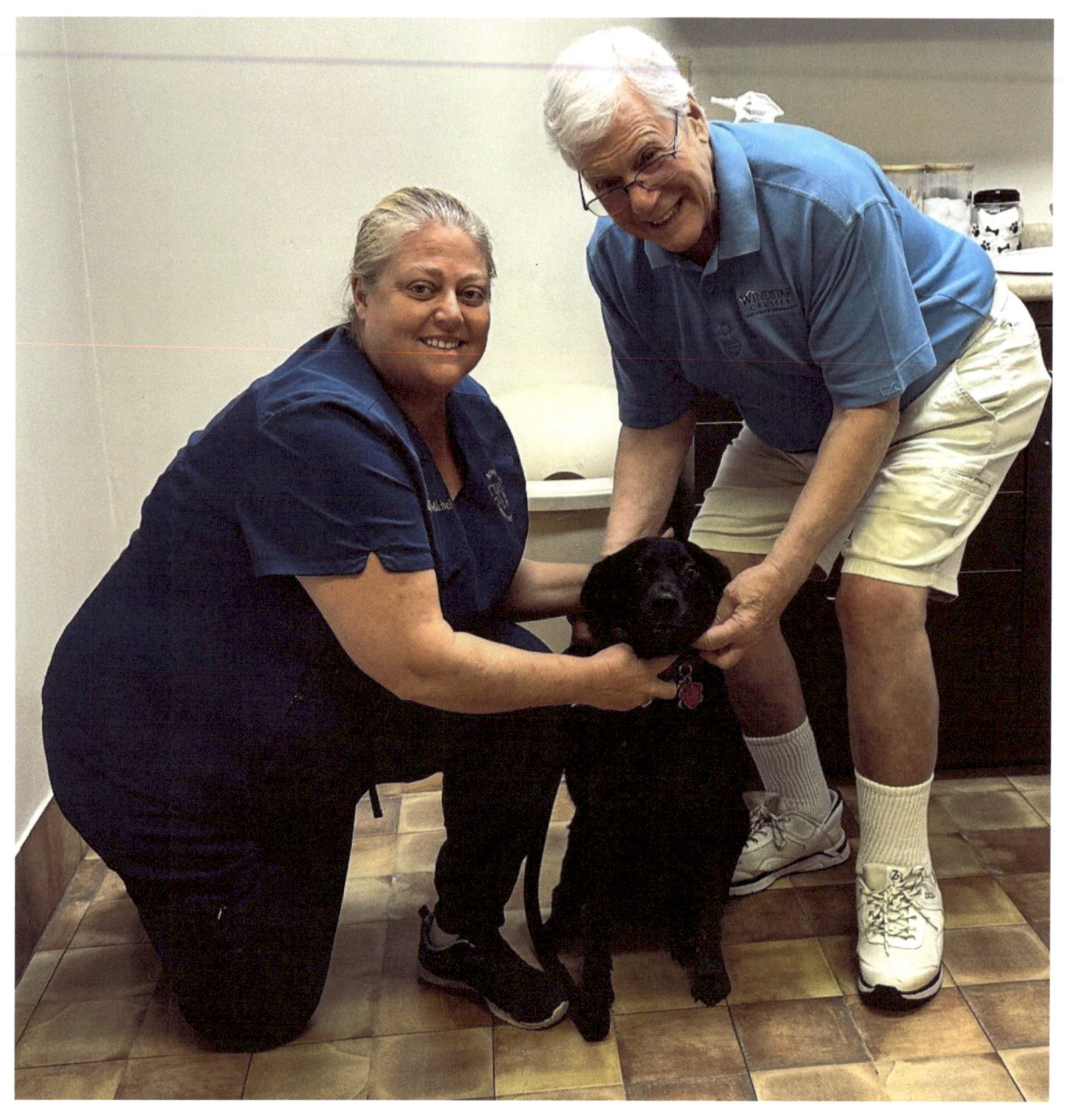

Dr. Shelly got me all checked out and approved, and she was pleased that I had lost a little weight! She said I would make a wonderful therapy dog!

Now it's time for me to train and prepare for my therapy dog evaluation – I am really excited and can't wait!

Chapter 3
I Start My Training!

To get started on my training, Dave and Marilyn left me with Jaime Benitez at **K9 Consultants** for three weeks while they went on a long vacation trip.

It was Jaime's job to provide food and shelter and also to teach some obedience lessons I will need for my therapy evaluations and therapy service.

I learned that I will be trained according to the Pet Partners Therapy Dog Training Plan, and Dave said the evaluation would be very similar to the American Kennel Club Canine Good Citizen Test.

Dave explained that "canine" means dog, and the "good citizen" part is about being able to obey 10 basic commands.

I already knew some obedience commands from Puppy Kindergarten, so I thought this would be easy. I was wrong – it didn't go like I thought it would.

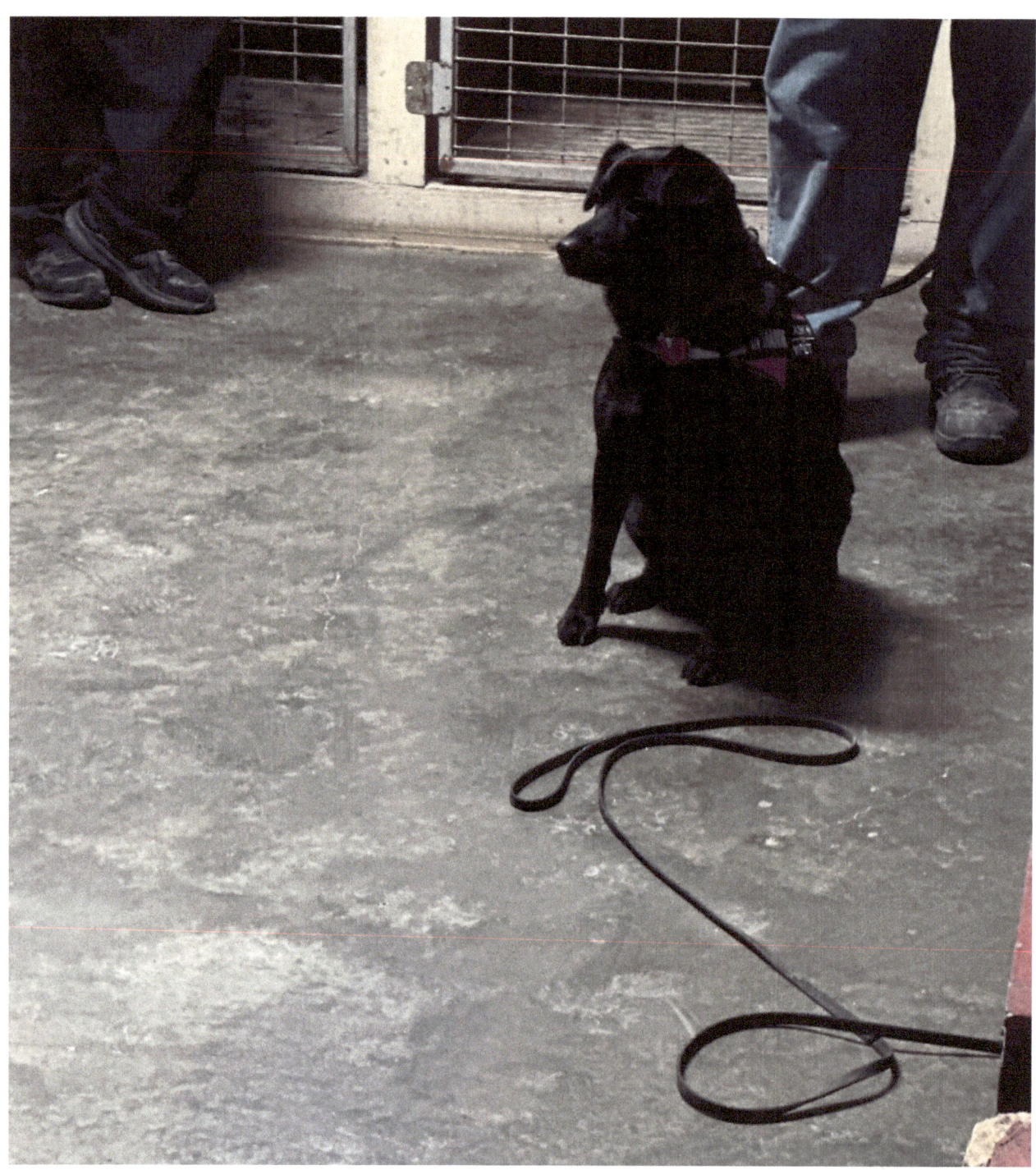

Chapter 4
This is Going to Be Harder Than I Thought!

There were a lot of dogs being trained at K9 Consultants – maybe 20 in all!

Most of these dogs were older than I am and seemed to know a lot more. They all seemed very smart and very confident, and I soon became a little nervous and afraid about how well I would do.

Many of these dogs also had something called "papers" that meant that all their parents and grandparents were the same kind of dog.

All my parents and grandparents were different types of dogs, so I felt like these dogs were probably better than me.

While some of the dogs were being trained to be therapy dogs, many of these dogs were being trained to be drug dogs for the U.S. Border Patrol. It takes a special type of dog to be able to do that, and they have to be really smart.

Several times these fancy dogs would look at me like "what are you doing here?" I began to wonder if I could compete with these dogs.

I learned that these dogs all came from special kennels and were expensive to buy. I came from a dirty ditch and was lucky to be taken to a forever home.

How could I ever compete with them?

Chapter 5

My Training, Week One

The first week with Jaime was not easy. All the other dogs seemed to be much better at taking commands. There were so many commands it was hard for me to remember them all. Fortunately, Jaime and his assistant Javier were very patient with me and kept repeating the commands until I could remember what to do.

I didn't want to fail my training and disappoint Dave and Marilyn.

I knew they would keep me if even I didn't pass, but I was afraid they would give up on training me for service.

I really want to serve, and I was starting to get scared.

Chapter 6
My Training, Week Two

During the second week of my training, things got better, and I could remember most of the commands.

Jaime and Javier complimented me on doing better and said that I would make a wonderful therapy dog.

I was relieved because I love people and really want to help people that are sick, lonely, or depressed.

I especially love children and hope to one day visit schools and classrooms.

By the end of the second week, I realized that I **really want** to do this – and that **I can** do this!

Chapter 7
I Start My Therapy Dog Evaluation

When Dave and Marilyn got back from their vacation trip and came to pick me up, Jaime gave the Pet Partners test to Dave and me.

The first thing I had to do was go up to a stranger and greet them. That was easy because I love people and love to meet them. What I had to remember was not to jump up on them, which I love to do when I greet people! Jaime said I'm too big to do that now and that I will knock people down! Not good!

Next I had to sit politely for petting. That was easy because I learned how to do that at Puppy Kindergarten and Dave has me sit every evening and pets me while he fixes my dinner.

Jaime also was evaluating Dave and paid as much attention to him as he did to me. He actually was giving Dave a score for each step just like me!

Next Jaime inspected my grooming and appearance which was also easy as I get a bath every weekend, and Dave trims and brushes my fur coat every week so it shines!

Then I walked with Dave on a leash around the training area. I think I went a little too fast because Jaime kept telling me to slow down.

I slowed down and walked right beside Dave, and then Jaime gave me a "thumbs up!"

Chapter 8

My Test is Going Well!

Next was walking through a crowd and staying with Dave. As I walked through the crowd with Dave, I saw many interesting people and things. I think I went slower than Jaime wanted, but he just smiled at me.

After that I had to go "sit" and "down" again which was easy because Dave has me do that every day.

Then Dave had to go about 15 feet away from me and call me to come to him. I wasn't paying attention and was a little slow to respond, so Jaime had me do this step over.   The next time Dave called I came immediately and got this step right!

The next step was to judge my reaction to other dogs I meet while working.

This is not easy for me because I never know how to act with strange dogs that I do not know. Will they be friendly?   Will they try to hurt me?   I hope I wasn't too shy, but I have to be careful.

Then Javier started dropping pans and tools and brooms making a bunch of sudden noises. Jaime explained to Dave that this part of the test was to see how I responded to several loud noises.

I didn't do much of anything – the noise just didn't bother me. Jaime smiled again and said I did great!

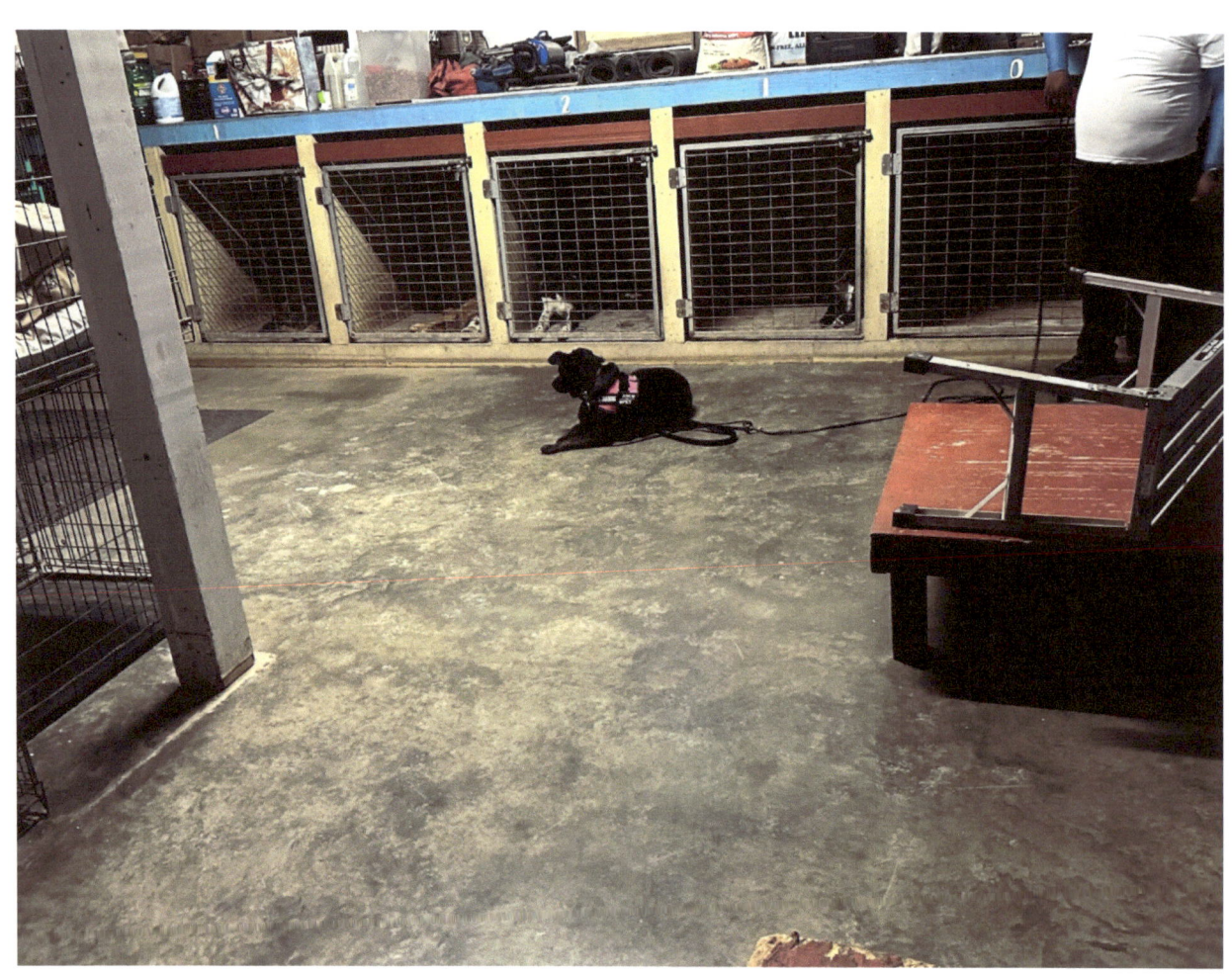

The final step was for Dave to have me wait for him and not move until he came back. This was new and hard for me to know what to do. Dave was gone almost three minutes, but I was right where he left me when he returned.

Chapter 9

We Passed the Test!

So the only thing I had to do over was the part where I had to come when called.

I paid attention to Dave and got it right the second time.

Jaime then looked at Dave and said, "You and Piper pass the Pet Partners Therapy Dog Team Evaluation!"

I was so relieved and so happy not to disappoint Dave and Marilyn and to be getting closer to doing what I think I was born to do – helping people!

Later that week Dave sent off the paperwork to Pet Partners to register us as a therapy team!

Now we have to find someone to give us a chance to be a therapy team!

Pet Partners Volunteer Registration Card

Registration Type: Handler Team Registration

Handler Name: Dave Osborn

Animal Name: Piper

Team Qualification Rating: Predictable

Special Qualifications, if any: none

Team Expiration Date: August 19, 2026

Chapter 10
Now for Our Therapy Visits!

The next step in our plan was to find locations that want to have therapy teams come and visit their patients and guests.

Pet Partners gives two levels of therapy animal registration – one is for quiet locations and lots of staff involvement like retirement homes and rehabilitation centers.

The other registration level is for noisy, busy hospitals and schools.

Dave and I will start with quiet locations for visits first. After we've had some experience with patients, we can begin going to schools and hospitals that encourage and allow therapy animals.

There are lots of rehabilitation centers, hospice centers for really sick people, retirement centers, and memory care centers where we live in the Rio Grande Valley in South Texas.

We will have plenty of opportunities to visit people who need us!

There are so many exciting things Dave and I will see. We will also meet some amazing people during our therapy visits – but that is another story!

Dave Osborn

As a retired technology chief executive officer, Dave is following a life-long passion for writing and has several projects in mind for future online and offline publications. He also has a passion for dogs so be sure to look for more books about his adventures with Piper, his companion and rescue dog.

Dave is also on the Board of the American Dog Society.

One of his favorite pastimes is sailing, and he holds both U.S. and International sailing certifications. Dave also enjoys South Texas bird hunting and bay fishing and is an avid grill master. Additionally, he is a bluegrass music fan and enjoys playing the piano, guitar, bass, and five-string banjo.

Dave holds a Bachelor of Science from Stephen F. Austin State University in Nacogdoches, Texas, and a Masters of Business Administration from Texas Christian University in Ft. Worth, Texas.

He resides in Harlingen, Texas, with his wife Marilyn and their rescue – and now therapy – dog Piper. They have two adult children and two grandsons who reside in the greater Houston area.

Books by Dave Osborn:

The Adventures of Piper: Book 1 Piper's Journey Home

The Adventures of Piper: Book 2 Piper Learns to Serve

Taking Charge!: 51 1/2 Years of Anecdotes and Advice for Aspiring Executives

Coming Soon:

The Adventures of Piper: Book 3 Piper On the Job

Signals of Deceit, an international thriller

Author's Acknowledgements

Again, while my name is on the cover, I owe a great debt of gratitude to:

- Marilyn Osborn, former Senior English teacher and later Dean of Students and Head of School, for her help in Piper's training and its reinforcement. She also is a great editor who helped with sentence structure and overall rhetoric.

- Jaime Osborn, first grade teacher and reading specialist extraordinaire, for her help in leveling **Piper Learns to Serve** at late 3rd/early 4th grade reading level. This includes vocabulary, sentence structure, and syntax.

- Matt and Dara Osborn, for their ongoing reviews, support, and edit suggestions.

- Jaime Benitez, owner of K9 Consultants, and his assistant Javier Lerna, for their outstanding care during Piper's boarding and the great training job they did with Piper.

- Dr. Shelly Mitchell, Piper's wonderful veterinarian, who always gives Piper good medical care and support.

- Pet Partners, Bellevue, Washington, for their great training programs and organizational support!

- And of course, Piper Osborn, now known as Lady Piper of Retama, best dog ever!

References

Reference is made to the American Kennel Club Canine Good Citizen Test. More specific information is available on the AKC website at:

https://www.akc.org/expert-advice/training/step-step-cgc-training/

Also, the Pet Partners is mentioned as a therapy animal sponsor. More information on Pet Partners is available on their website at:

https://petpartners.org/

www.ingramcontent.com/pod-product-compliance
Lightning Source LLC
Chambersburg PA
CBHW040725060526
44119CB00083B/333